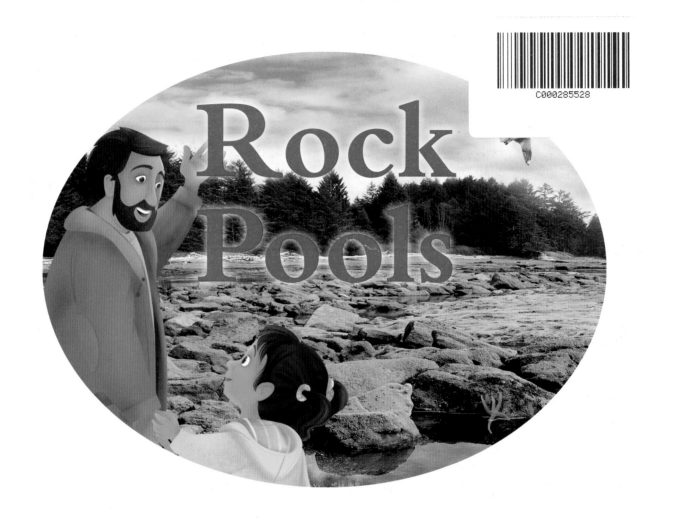

Rock Pools

Written by Catherine Baker

Illustrated by Ángeles Peinador

Collins

C000285528

Rock pools are full of cool things!

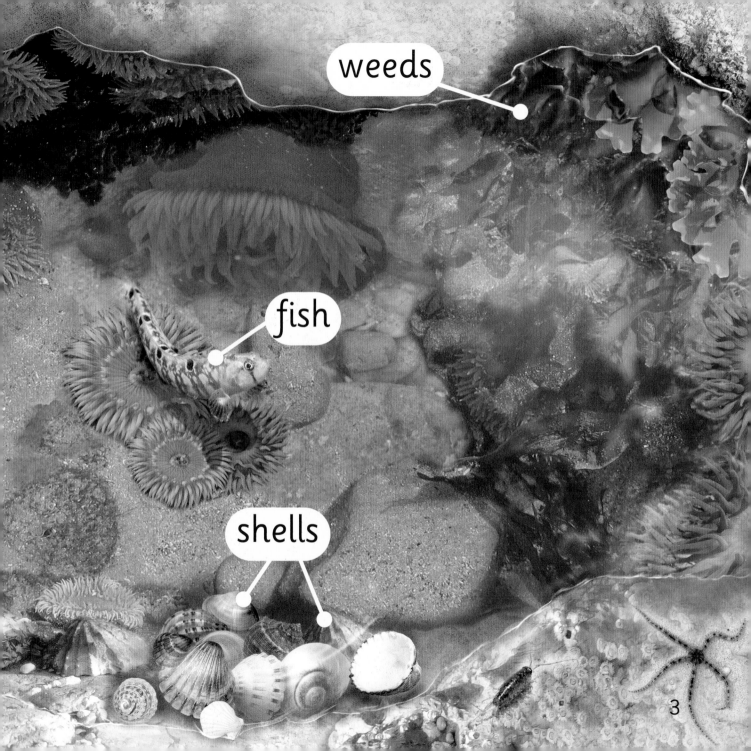

weeds

fish

shells

3

Get a bucket, boots and a coat.

Look for things in this weed.

gutweed

This fish is long and thin.

8

You might see lots of shells.

This shell can run!

A hermit is in it.

hermit

Look in this rock pool!

🐾 Review: After reading 🐾

Use your assessment from hearing the children read to choose any GPCs, words or tricky words that need additional practice.

Read 1: Decoding

- Remind the children that "oo" can make two different sounds. Ask the children to sound out, then blend these words, choosing the correct sound:

  p/oo/l/s   c/oo/l   l/oo/k   b/oo/t/s

- Challenge the children to sound out and blend words that contain long vowel sounds. Can they point to the two- or three-letter graphemes in each word?

  r/ai/n   c/oa/t   m/igh/t   g/u/t/w/ee/d   h/er/m/i/t

Read 2: Prosody

- Model reading each page with expression to the children. After you have read each page, ask the children to have a go at reading with expression.
- On pages 5 and 9, show the children how to invent a girl's voice for the speech bubbles.

Read 3: Comprehension

- Turn to pages 14 and 15. Use the picture to recap on what you can find in a rock pool. Encourage the children to identify and describe as many things as possible.
- For every question ask the children how they know the answer. Ask:
  o What does the book say we should we do if we think it might rain? (*get a coat*)
  o What things can you find in a rock pool? (e.g. *weeds, fish, limpets, mussels, shells*)
  o What did the girl find that was long and thin? (*a fish*)
  o What sort of shells might you find in a rock pool? (*mussels, limpets, a shell with a hermit in it*)
  o Why does the shell run on page 13? (*a hermit is in it*)
- Ask the children what their favourite part of the book was, and to explain why.